MAKE AND CREATE
SPOON ANIMALS
AND
PEN TOPPERS

Picture Credits: Includes photographs by

Photodisc, Corel, Ingram Publishing and Top That! Photography.

Published by Top That! Publishing plc
Tide Mill Way, Woodbridge, Suffolk, IP12 1AP, UK
www.topthatpublishing.com

Spoon Animals Getting Started

Get ready to turn ordinary wooden spoons into fantastic wild animals!

Just follow the illustrated step-by-step instructions to make an elephant and a lion. To make your spoon animal friends you will need a range of craft items, including colored felt, goggle eyes, glue, wool and of course, wooden spoons! All of these items can either be found around the home or bought easily and cheaply from craft and hobby stores. The items needed for each project are listed at the beginning, so make sure you have all of the items before you start.

Top Tips

- Paint the spoons to match the animals' color.

- Draw the shapes in pencil before you cut them out.

- Make the most of your felt pieces by cutting shapes out close together.

- Keep your felt offcuts to use for ears, eyes and noses!

- If you run out of felt, you could use material scraps, colored paper or paint to complete your animals.

- To make matching ears, cut one out and use it as a template to draw round.

- If you can't find any goggle eyes, simply use colored felt or card in their place.

- Remember, making great craft projects is fun. If you can't find any items try and think of an alternative, or why not try creating your own animal designs.

Ebo the Elephant

You will need:
A spoon
1 piece of light gray felt
A pencil and a black felt pen
Glue and scissors
2 pieces of dark gray felt
1 piece of white felt
2 goggle eyes

1. Place the spoon on the light gray felt and draw around it with a pencil, as shown below. Cut out the shape and glue it to the flat side of the spoon.

2. Now cut a piece of dark gray felt in half.

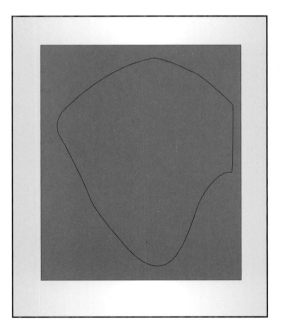

3. Draw an ear shape onto one of the dark gray halves, as shown above, and cut it out.

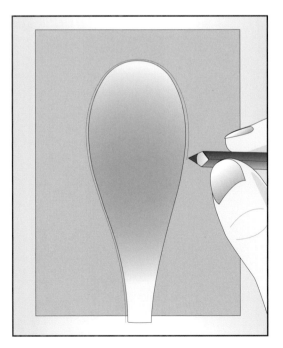

4. Using the cut-out ear as a template, draw a second ear on the remaining felt half, as shown right. Cut it out. Turn the spoon over and arrange the ears on either side of the elephant's head.

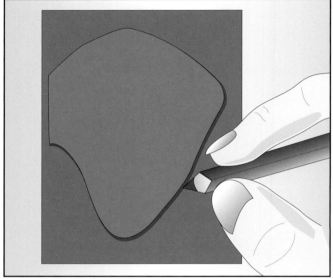

5. Glue the straight edges of the ears to the back of the spoon, as below.

6. Draw the trunk shape, as shown below, onto the other piece of dark gray felt. Cut it out and then glue the top half of the trunk onto the front of the spoon.

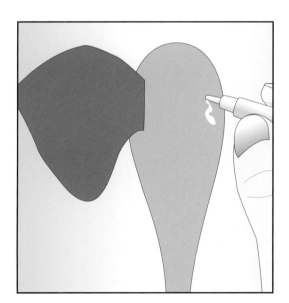

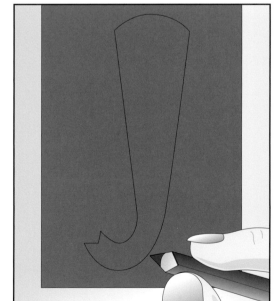

7. Draw a tusk shape onto the white felt, as shown right, and cut it out. Draw around this shape and cut out a second tusk. Flip one of the tusks over so that both curve inwards, and glue just the tops to either side of the widest part of the trunk.

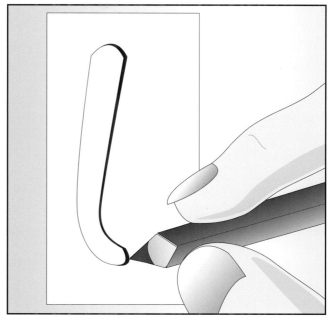

8. Glue the eyes onto dark gray felt and cut around them. Stick the eyes onto the elephant's face.

9. To finish, add some wrinkles onto the trunk using a felt pen.

Lisimba the Lion

You will need:
A spoon
1 piece of yellow felt
5 ft brown wool
A pencil and a black felt pen
Glue and scissors
1 piece of orange felt
1 piece of black felt
1 piece of brown felt
2 goggle eyes

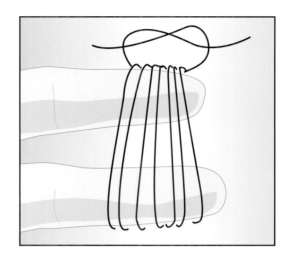

1. Place the spoon on the yellow felt and draw around it with a pencil, as below. Cut out the shape and glue it to the flat side of the spoon.

2. Cut a 6 in. piece of wool, and then wind the rest around two fingers. Carefully slide the looped section off your fingers, then thread the short piece through the top and knot it.

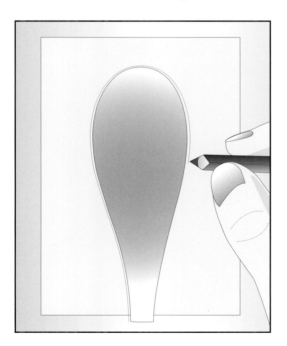

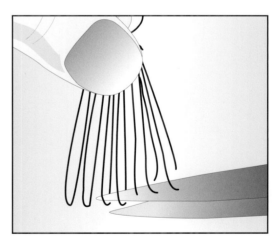

3. Carefully cut through the loops at the unknotted end.

4. Squeeze a blob of glue onto the middle of the back of the spoon. Take the wool from step 3, and stick down the knotted end. Leave it to dry. Separate the wool strands out to create an even mane. Glue the strands into place, as shown right.

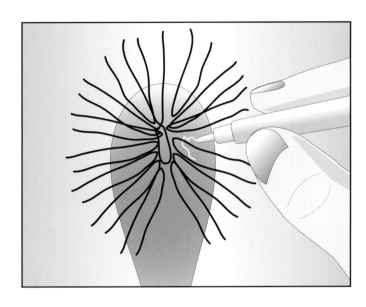

5. Cut the orange felt into two 1 1/2 x 4 in. strips. Make snips along the strips to form the mane, as below.

6. Glue the mane on top of the wool section, as below. Fan out the strips so that they spread evenly around the spoon edge.

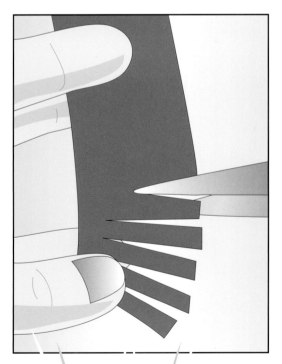

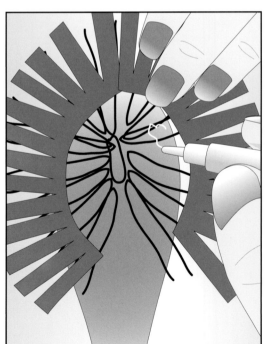

7. To make the ears, cut two circles, 1/2 in. wide, from the yellow felt. Then, cut two smaller circles from the orange felt so they just fit inside the larger yellow circles. Trim the orange circles into the inner ear shapes, as shown right. Glue the ear pieces together, and then glue them to the lion's head, as shown right.

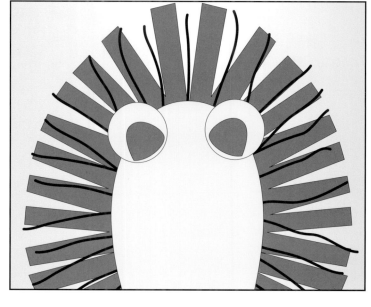

9. Glue the eyes onto brown felt and cut around them, leaving a narrow border. Stick on the eyes and nose, then add the whiskers and mouth with black felt pen.

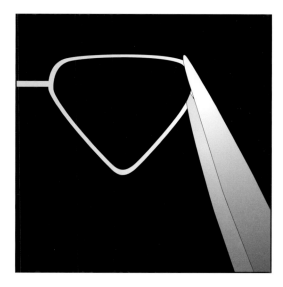

8. Cut the lion's nose out of black felt into the triangular shape shown above.

Pen Toppers
Getting Started

**There will be a party in your pencil case
once you've made these pen pals!**

From a frog to a flower and pig, the illustrated steps on the following pages make creating fun pen toppers easy! You will need a range of craft items which can be found in craft and hobby stores. Items you will need include pompoms, fuzzy sticks, beads, goggle eyes and colored felt, all of which are listed at the beginning of each project. You will also need some everyday items such as glue, tape and pens and pencils. Remember, once you have completed the projects on the following pages, you can have great fun creating your own pen toppers!

Before making your pen toppers, try practicing the two techniques below on some spare craft items. This will make sure your finished projects look really professional!

SPIRALLING

Wind a fuzzy stick around a pencil to get a perfect spiral shape.

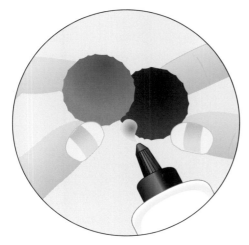

GLUING POMPOMS

Hold glued pompoms together for at least 30 seconds, to make sure they are stuck together.

If you can't find all of the items listed for each project, try thinking up fun alternatives to make the pen toppers your own!

FUNKY FROG

**Forget the lily pad—
Funky Frog prefers your pen top!**

YOU WILL NEED:

- black embroidery thread
- scissors
- 1 dark green pompom
- glue

- 1 light green fuzzy stick
- 1 dark green fuzzy stick
- 2 light green pompoms
- 2 goggle eyes
- a pen or pencil

1. To make the mouth, cut a length of black thread measuring 1/2 in. Glue it in a U-shape to the middle of the dark green pompom, as shown.

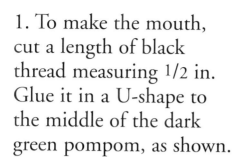

2. Now cut a 1/2 in. length of light green fuzzy stick and bend it into a V-shape. Glue it to the base of the dark green pompom to form the front legs.

3. To form the back legs, cut the dark green fuzzy stick in half. Bend and shape each piece so you have a curved shape with a webbed foot at the end, as shown left. The foot shape can be formed by folding the fuzzy stick back on itself.

4. Glue the bendy legs made in step 3 onto the base of the dark green pompom, with them sitting to the side, as shown right.

5. Take the two light green pompoms and glue a goggle eye onto each. Allow these to dry, and then glue the two light green pompoms onto the top of the dark green pompom.

6. Finally, take the remaining piece of light green fuzzy stick, bend the end over, and glue this to the base of the dark green pompom. Now wind the rest around your pen or pencil to hold the frog in place.

FLOWER POWER

Add a summer feelin' to your pen with these fabulous flowers.

YOU WILL NEED:

- white card
- scissors
- 1 green fuzzy stick
- glue
- 2 small blue pompoms
- 12 small pink pompoms
- a pen or pencil

1. Cut out a circle from the white card measuring 1 1/2 in. in diameter. Now glue one end of the green fuzzy stick to one side of the circle. This will form the base and stem of the flower.

TOP TIP!

Make lots of different-colored flowers for all of your friends—just choose their favorite colors. These fun pen toppers will make great birthday or Christmas gifts!

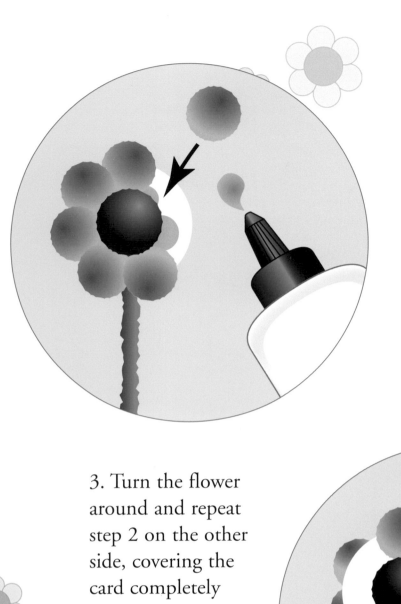

2. Completely cover the same side of the circle with glue. Glue a blue pompom in the middle and a ring of six pink pompoms around it. Allow to dry thoroughly before moving on to the next step.

3. Turn the flower around and repeat step 2 on the other side, covering the card completely with pompoms. Again, allow to dry thoroughly.

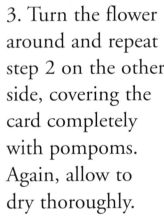

4. Approximately 2¼ in. below the flower, bend the green fuzzy stick stem into the shape of a leaf, holding it in place with a twist, as shown right. This can be tidied up once you have attached the flower to your pen.

5. Finally, wind the stem of your funky flower around your pen or pencil.

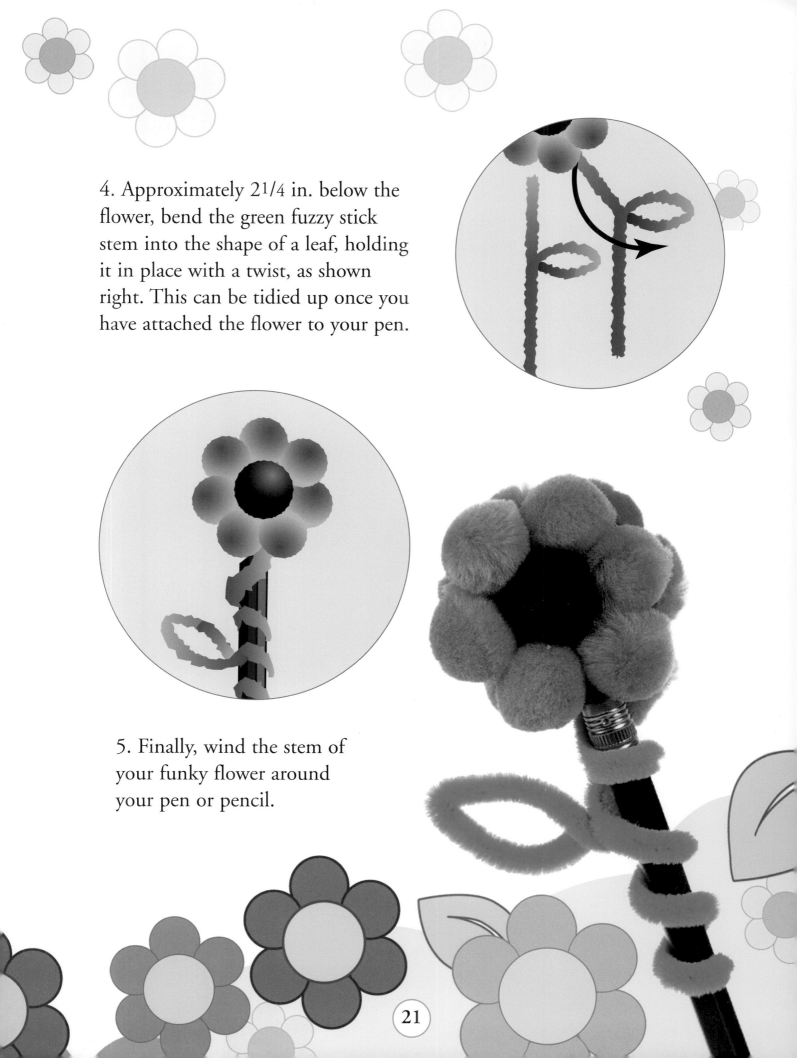

PERFECT PIGGY

This cute little piggy makes a perfect pen topper.

YOU WILL NEED:

- 1 extra large pink pompom
- 1 medium pink pompom
- glue
- a piece of pink felt
- scissors
- 1 small pink pompom
- a black felt pen
- 1 pink fuzzy stick
- 2 goggle eyes
- a pen or pencil

1. Glue the medium pink pompom onto the extra large pompom to make the head and body shape, as shown.

2. Make the pig's snout by attaching a small piece of oval felt to the small pink pompom, then glue this pompom to the front of the head. Use a black felt pen to draw on two nostrils.

3. From the felt, cut out two small triangles for ears and four trotter shapes (see step 4 for a guide to their shape). Glue on the ears.

4. Cut the pink fuzzy stick into four small pieces to form legs. Glue the four felt trotters to the ends of the fuzzy sticks and then glue them to the body, as shown.

5. Glue the goggle eyes onto the head. Finally, glue a fuzzy stick to the base of the pig's body. Wind the fuzzy stick around a pen or pencil once the glue is dry.